SO-AXN-321

Free Weaving
on frame and loom

Free Weaving
on frame and loom

ELISABETH HOPPE
ESTINE OSTLUND
LISA MELEN

VAN NOSTRAND REINHOLD COMPANY
New York   Cincinnati   Toronto   London   Melbourne

Van Nostrand Reinhold Company
Regional Offices:
New York Cincinnati Chicago Millbrae Dallas

Van Nostrand Reinhold Company
International Offices:
London Toronto Melbourne

This book was originally published in Swedish
under the title of *Väva Fritt* by ICA Forlaget AB.
Vasteras, Sweden.

Copyright © for *Väva Fritt* ICA Forlaget AB,
1972. English translation ©
Van Nostrand Reinhold Company Ltd. 1974.

Translated from the Swedish by Mats Wiktorsson

Library of Congress Catalog Card Number
73-16707
ISBN 0 442 30038 7 Cl
0 442 30039 5 Pb

All rights reserved. No part of this work covered
by the copyright hereon may be reproduced or
used in any form or by any means – graphic,
electronic, or mechanical, including
photocopying, recording, taping, or
information storage and retrieval systems –
without written permission of the publisher.

This book is filmset in Univers and printed in
Great Britain by Jolly & Barber Ltd, Rugby.

Published by Van Nostrand Reinhold Company Inc.,
450 West 33rd Street, New York, N.Y. 10001 and
Van Nostrand Reinhold Company Ltd.
25-28 Buckingham Gate, London SW1E 6LQ.

16 15 14 13 12 11 10 9 8 7 6 5 4 3 2 1

Library of Congress Cataloging in Publication Data
Hoppe, Elisabeth, 1915–
  Free weaving on frame and loom.
  Translation of Väva fritt i ram och vävstol.
  1. Hand weaving. I. Östlund, Estine, 1924–
II. Melén. Lisa, 1917–   III. Title.
TT848.H613   746.1'4   73-16707
ISBN 0–442–30038–7
ISBN 0–442–30039–5 (pbk.)

Contents

Weaving looms and weaving frames 7

Pattern making 26

Colour 31

Weaving techniques with variations 39
  Cottolin weaves 39
  Woollen weaves 42
  Double weave on a small loom 46
  One warp — many weaves 48
  The MMF technique 51
  Variations on a 'rose path' theme 57
  Weft picked damask 60
  Double weaves 61

Ideas for patterns 68

Techniques 85

Glossary of weaves 88

List of Suppliers 89

Index 90

Weaving looms and weaving frames

Lisa Melén

Weaving looms

There are several kinds of small and large looms on the market. It may be useful to have a loom which is collapsible and portable, for easy transportation after a weaving class. Most loom manufacturers produce standard small looms with an internal width of about 27—40 in. (60—80 cm.). (See illustration on the left.)

The illustration below shows a collapsible loom set up for use. As you can see, the collapsible loom requires little space when folded. Looms equipped with adjustable pedals for children are also available.

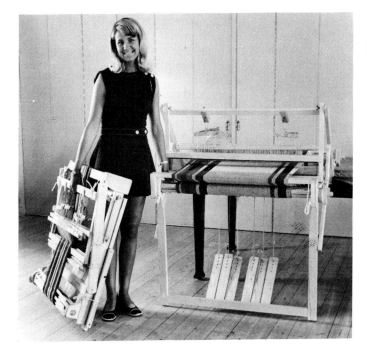

(Opposite) Weaving loom with four shafts and six pedals.
(Left) Collapsible loom.

7

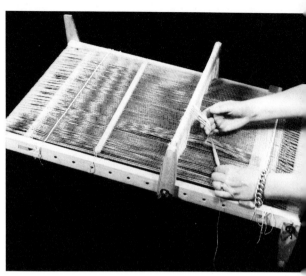

(Left) Weaving frame. (Right) Weaving frame with weft.

Weaving frames

When a patterned weave is required such as tapestry weave, special Swedish weaves like *röllakan* or the HV technique, or double weave (Finnish weave), you can weave on either a weaving frame or a tapestry loom. For beginners and for weaving smaller pieces of work, the single weaving frame is the most appropriate. It is light, easily transportable, and simple to use.

One of the most common frames on the market is about 24 in. (50 cm.) wide and 30 in. (70 cm.) high. (See the illustration on the left.) There are also larger frames, frames with special weft arrangements, and frames arranged so that the warp can be pulled forward during the weaving process. (See illustration on the right, above.)

If larger pieces of work are required the vertical tapestry loom is the obvious choice. See the illustration on p. 9.

The simplest type of frame to assemble is the 'Elisabeth frame', which consists of two vertical round heddles with slots for two bars. See the illustration on p. 9, above left.

To set up the warp, you wind the warp threads over the bars, and then put a chain of stitches at the top and bottom of the frame so that the distance between the threads is equal. (See the illustration opposite, below left.)

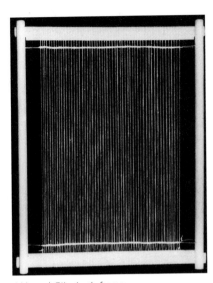

(Above) Elisabeth frame.

(Left) Make sure that you put down the chain to regulate the distance between the warp threads. Crochet the threads two and two together. (See p. 25.)

(Above) Vertical tapestry loom.

When the weaving process is completed the work should remain in the frame. In this way it is already mounted.

A key frame (artist's frame) can also be used. In this frame the warp is threaded in the same way as in the Elisabeth frame. When the work is finished you remove the keys and take the work out of the frame. The remaining warp threads, which are not cut off, form fringes at the top and bottom of the frame.

Yarn calculation

Before you set up a weave, you must determine the proper width and length, the thickness of the yarn, and the appropriate reed. The warp length consists of:
(1)   the required finished length
(2)   the take-up, which is approximately 10% of the above
(3)   approximately 16 in. (40 cm.) up to the selvedge (the end section of the warp cannot be woven on)
(4)   approximately 4–6 in. (10–15 cm.) for tying
    You can now calculate the number of threads across the entire width. This is done by multiplying the density of the reed by the width of the reed, then multiplying this product by the number of threads required on the reed. The easiest way to calculate the amount of yarn needed is to calculate its weight, i.e. the length of the warp multiplied by the number of warp yarns in width, divided by the count number multiplied by the yarn number. Thus:

$$\frac{\text{warp length} \times \text{number of warp threads in width} \times \text{number of plies}}{\text{count number} \times \text{standard number}}$$

= yarn consumption.
There is an international agreement between Continental yarn manufacturers that the count number should always be the length in metres of a one-ply yarn per kilo of weight. This system is being introduced in the U.S. and U.K.

    Here are the count numbers for some common yarns:

cotton yarn	1600
linen yarn unbleached	560
linen yarn semi-bleached and dyed	650
linen yarn bleached	700
woollen yarn	1000
cotton carpet warp	1400
linen carpet warp	560
cottolin unbleached	580
(i.e. a mixture of linen and cotton)	
cottolin bleached and dyed	650
hemp yarn	470

    To calculate the length of the warp from a given weight of yarn and a given number of threads in width, multiply the weight by the count number and the standard number, and then divide the product by the number of threads multiplied by the number of plies. Thus:

10

$$\frac{\text{weight} \times \text{count number} \times \text{standard number}}{\text{number of threads} \times \text{number of plies}} = \text{warp length.}$$

To calculate the number of threads across the entire width from a given weight of yarn and a given length of warp, multiply the weight by the count number and the yarn number, and then divide the product by the number of plies multiplied by the length. Thus:

$$\frac{\text{weight} \times \text{count number} \times \text{standard number}}{\text{length} \times \text{number of plies}} = \text{number of threads.}$$

To calculate the amount of yarn needed in the weft, multiply the weft threads per cm. (about $\frac{3}{8}$ in.) by the width of the reed, the length of the cloth, and the number of plies and divide the product by the standard number multiplied by the count number. Thus:

$$\frac{\text{weft threads per cm.} \times \text{width of reed} \times \text{length of cloth} \times \text{number of plies}}{\text{standard number} \times \text{count number}}$$

$= \text{weight.}$

Setting up the weave

The first step in setting up a weave is to warp, i.e. to arrange the warp yarns according to a given length and a given number of threads. Most types of yarn are now available on spools, but yarns sold in skeins must first be wound on to bobbins before they are used. This is done by putting the skeins first on to the warping mill, and then winding them on to the bobbins. These bobbins are manufactured in both wood and metal. A simple way of obtaining the right length of warp is to measure a piece of string the same length as the finished warp. Attach the string to the stick that protrudes furthest at the warp shed and wind the warping mill as many times as it takes to arrive at the end of the string. Put the last stick in the nearest hole in the warping mill and fasten the string securely to the stick. (Leave the string on the warping mill until the warping is completed.)

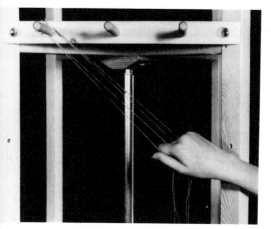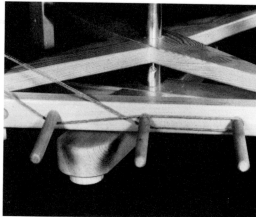

(Left) Warping with four threads. (Right) The threads crossing in the shed.

You should warp with 2–4 threads. Let the threads run parallel and tie them together to make what is known as a group. Wind the group over the top peg and then pass it round the warping mill continuously, following the string, until you reach the required length. (See the illustration above left.) The threads cross at the bottom of the shed sticks (see illustration above right), forming a figure-eight. Hold the threads firmly and evenly throughout the entire warping process, and wind them tightly on top when you go down and tightly at the bottom when you go up. The warping must be done continuously, otherwise it can easily become uneven.

Wide warp plaits can be warped in two or more sections to make sure that they are completely even. Count the threads at the bottom of the shed, and at the same time secure them firmly in several places on either side of the shed. (See the illustration on p. 13, left.) If you have a large number of threads you can make the work easier by counting 50–100 threads and tying a piece of yarn in a contrasting colour round them.

Tie up the warp each time as well as at the last stick. When you remove the warp plait from the warping mill, begin by loosening it at the top and taking out the last stick. Pull the warp through the loop which has been formed in such a way that you get a new loop. (See the illustaration on p. 13, right.) Now you plait it, alternating your left and right hands. You cannot pull the end of the warp plait through the very last loop, so instead tie a piece of strong string round it, approximately $3\frac{3}{4}$ in. (9 cm.) from the end.

(Left) The shed is wound round.
(Right) The warp lengths are twisted down.

Spreading

The aim of spreading is to obtain the right width of warp plait in the loom. This is most easily done directly behind the loom, in a reed which is usually half the density of the one used for weaving. (If you use a thick reed for weaving, you can obviously use the same one for spreading.) If you have warped with two threads, four threads should run together during each threading. If you have warped with four threads, eight threads should run together, and so on. So you must work out how many threadings the number of warp threads needs, and distribute the number of dents evenly in the width of the reed. We may take the example of the linen curtain on p. 57. Number of threads: 704. Number of threadings: 704 ÷ 4 = 176 threadings. Width of the reed: 7½ in. (18 cm.). Reed: 35/10 = 350 dents, 350 dents ÷ 176 threadings = 2 (every other dent). The exact number of dents will be 352, thus giving two dents for each threading, which is an advantage in spreading.

Remove the heddle rods in the loom and tie the warp plait on to the crosspiece bar. Place two chairs behind the loom, and pull the warp over to them. Put one shed stick into each shed, tie the sticks together, then tie them to the armrests of the chairs. Place the reed on the armrests and spread by using a reed hook, putting each group into the dents in the same order as round the shed sticks. (See the illustration on p. 14, left.) Remember that the threads should lie in the centre.

13

(Left) Spreading. (Right) The threads are passed on to a stick.

Pass the groups of threads on to a stick, which should lie in the same shed as the nearest shed stick. (See the illustration above right.)

Pulling on the warp or beaming

Pass the warp threads over to the stick of the warp beam, and distribute cotton strings between the warp threads so that you can centre the warp in the reed. Take out the middle, and measure the same distance between the holes in the warp beam as in the warp. Remove all the strings and hold them in one hand, then slot the beam stick into the warp and put the strings at the appropriate places in the warp. Check carefully that the warp is in the centre of the loom and that none of the groups is twisted.

Changing the shed

Remove the leash stick A, which is nearest to the reed. (See the illustration on p. 15, right.) Hold the remaining stick B in a vertical position against the reed and pull the leash stick A into the shed which has been formed on the other side of the reed. (See the illustration on p. 16, top left.)

14

Remove the first stick and pull it into the shed which has been formed nearest to the warp beam. (See the illustration on p. 16, top right.) Tie the leash sticks together and stretch the warp. Check again that the warp is straight in the loom, and start pulling. (See the illustration on p. 16, bottom left.) It is advisable to have two people pulling on the warp. One of them can keep the warp plait stretched, while the other pulls on the warp, places the warp ribs, keeps the leash sticks together, and keeps the warp stretched evenly. The ribs can now be put down (leaving a gap of one rib between them the first time) as protection against the hard warp strings of the beam. Then it is easy to put the new ribs in to the gaps the second time. Pull three or four times, then repeat the entire process. Pull the warp plait until you are left with about 27 in. (60 cm.). Now tie the shed sticks to the stretcher rod.

Remove the warp from the reed and tie the threads to the leash stick in small bundles, using running loops which are easy to untie. Put the leash sticks in a convenient place.

(Left) The warp threads are transferred to the stick of the warp beam.
(Right) Leash stick A, which is nearest to the reed, is removed.

(Left) Stick B is placed horizontally against the reed and stick A is
pulled through the shed that has been formed on the other side. (Right)
Stick B is removed and threaded into the shed nearest the warp beam.

Leashing or threading

Place the leash, which must be as long as the heddle bars, with
the knot hanging down. Always leash from right to left. Holding
the leash in your left hand, use your right hand to pull the warp

(Left) The leash sticks are tied together and the warp is stretched.
(Right) Leashing.

(Above) Wall decoration. (Below) Tjörn, a beach. Woven on a loom.
(See the description on p. 59.) Designed and woven by Estine Östlund.

(Above) Picked damask. (See the description on p. 60.) (Below)
Autumn leaf woven in the transparent technique. (See frottage, p. 79.)
Only the pattern pieces are woven. Designed and woven by
Estine Östlund.

threads through the eye of the leash. (See the illustration below right.)

Leash the threads in the order in which they lie in the shed. Having leashed a section on the draft plan, tie the threads together. Follow the part of the draft plan where the shaft is nearest to the warp beam, so that the last shaft is nearest to you. If there is one dash or one square on the plan, there will be one thread in the leash; if there are two dashes on the same shaft, there will also be two threads in the leash, and so on.

(Left) Sleying. (Right) The reed is passed through the warp beam.

Sleying (passing the warp through the reed)

You should also sley from right to left. Hang the reed in front of the shaft, put the threads on to the reed, and pull them through the dents with a reed hook. (See the illustration above left.) The threads must be arranged in the same order in which they were leashed, and must not cross each other. When you have sleyed a bundle of threads, tie them together. When you leash, be careful not to end up with empty dents; missed dents will leave bad flaws in the weave. Place the reed in the beater and check that the warp is in the centre of the loom. (See the illustration above right.) Tie the leash sticks loosely, but make sure that they are securely tied to the stretcher rod.

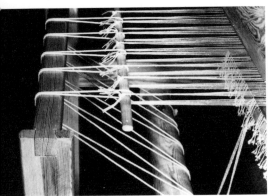
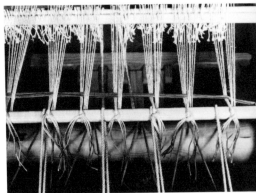

(Left) A beam stick is threaded into the strings of the warp beam and up against the reed. (Right) Stretch a cord between the groups of yarns to make the warp threads even.

Thread a beam stick into the strings of the warp beam so that it comes up from below over the knee beam, in front of the breast beam, and up against the reed. (See the illustration above left.) See that the strings are evenly distributed along the beam stick

The warp threads are tied firmly to the stick.

by measuring the stick and placing the centre string in the middle. Measure the distance between the holes on the warp beam and leave the same distance between each string along the stick. Tie the warp threads by taking a group of yarns and dividing it into two equal parts; put half of the string over the stick and the other half under the stick, and tie them up in the centre. Then pick up the right-hand group and put it diagonally across the knot, below the upper group, and then down. Check carefully that all the knots are evenly stretched and tie an overhand knot. (See the illustration opposite below.)

Top-tying

Put the warp threads in the bottom part of the leash eye. Measure the distance between the side-rests, divide this into four equal parts, and place the pulleys of the heddle pole (or strings to keep the heddle horses in position) a quarter of the distance from the side-rests. Join the heddle horses with shafts and with bundles of leash consisting of six leashes to a bundle. (See the illustration on p. 22.)

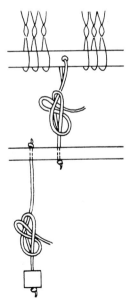

Under-tying. Tie the shaft sticks to the lever/pedal.

Under-tying (tying up the pedals)

When you are weaving with two shafts, they should be tied directly to the pedals. If you are weaving with several shafts, it is advisable to use levers. In this case each shaft must be tied to a lever and the pedal must be tied so that it is in a strictly horizontal position below the lever. (See the illustration.) Tie the shafts and levers to the pedal with a treadle knot. Place a plan for tying the pedals so that it can be read up and down easily during tying-up; for weaving it must be placed with the right side up. Each blacked-out square indicates a piece of string and each vertical square a pedal. Read carefully, starting from your right. If two squares are blacked out there are two pieces of string to each pedal.

Practical advice

Before you begin weaving check the beater, which should be placed evenly at each end and just high enough for the warp to

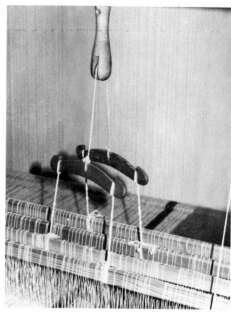

(Left) Top-tying with 2 shafts. (Right) Top-tying with 4 shafts.

be in the centre of the reed. You should also check that the shafts and pedals are standing evenly and are held up just high enough. The warp must run straight through from the stretcher rod (or warp beam) to the breast beam, and must rest in the bottom part of the leash eye, as well as passing through the middle of the reed. (This process is described from the side of the loom.) Tighten the weave and pull through the yarn which was left over during the first weft; at the same time check that the leashing and sleying are working correctly. (Make sure that the density of the weft is right. If the warp and weft yarns are equally thick, it is advisable to weave the warp and weft with equal density.) If a warp thread breaks, it is essential to mend it immediately: repair the damage with a weaving knot or a sailor knot, pin the thread to the fabric, and when the weaving process is complete, thread it by wrapping it over in the direction of the warp.

A tenter is very useful for elastic materials like wool, and in cases where it is difficult to retain the width of the weave. Otherwise you will have to leave it.

Finishing processes for wool weaves

When you are weaving wool, it is the finishing process which gives the weave its final appearance. Only in exceptional cases can you do this for yourself: the material is usually sent out to a specialist. However, as you will naturally want the final effect to be as attractive as possible, some advice is given below as to what your weave should look like, so that the specialist you send it to can produce satisfactory work.

● Always use high quality woollen yarn with a run-proof colour.

● Check that the weave is properly finished off. All knots must be untied and the threads threaded in a wrapover manner approximately $\frac{3}{4}$ in. (2 cm.) from the ends. Loose threads on selvedges, etc. must be cut off. Any flaws in the weaving can be corrected, with the use of a mending needle.

● Fringes are most easily made in the loom in the following way: leave a warp approximately 10 in. (25 cm.) long with no weft shots and then go on to weave the next plaid, scarf, or shawl. After this, twist together four threads at a time in the same direction, then twist them in the opposite direction. When you are twisting them together slot two double woollen yarns into the fringe

● Do not cut the weave, but let it hang together; this giver a better result as well as being more economical.

● Fold the weave into large, soft pleats and roll up only the very last metre or so, so that the weave stays together.

● Include in your parcel an order letter, with your name and address clearly written. To help the specialist you should give him as much information as possible as to the purpose of the weave, the required finished width of plaids, shawls, and scarves, and so on. If you are not sure about anything it is always best to contact the finisher.

One example of a finishing process is moth-proofing. If you use only well-known brands of washed and dyed yarn there is no need to worry about this as these are already moth-proofed. Unwashed yarns, however, are not usually treated against moths, nor are home-made yarns, which are becoming more and more popular. In these cases you must instruct the finisher to moth-proof the cloth. The process does not affect the appearance or condition of the weave in any way, but it does give effective protection against moths during the entire lifetime of the cloth.

Warping in the frame

The width of the warp is calculated according to the width of the pattern. The most commonly used nail frame has 25 nails, and thus 50 threads per cm. ($\frac{3}{8}$ in.). This type of warp density is suitable for linen yarn 11/5. It is best to keep the thread on a spool when you warp. Stretch the warp threads between the nails, which are arranged in groups, to facilitate counting. Stretch the warp yarns tightly and evenly. If you require a

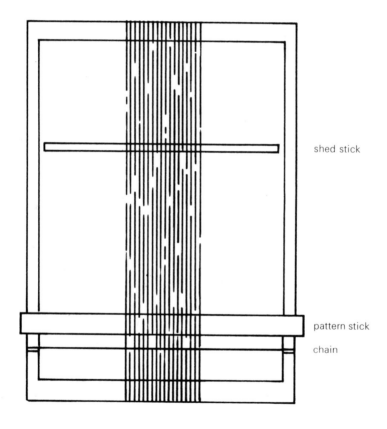

shed stick

pattern stick

chain

Frame ready for weaving.

coarser warp, for example 8/2, you must warp much more loosely. You then warp round four nails, leaving the fifth, and so on. You regulate the distance between the warp threads with the chain. You have now obtained a density in the warp of 40 threads per cm. ($\frac{3}{8}$ in.), which is appropriate for coarser wefts. We have used this density in the warp for the 'film weave' in the frame illustrated on p. 66. Sometimes the pattern is woven with the frame lying flat while you are working on it. The finished tapestry will then be the width of the frame. It is important to remember this when you calculate the width of the warp. You must also remember to keep the warp in the centre of the frame. This is a more comfortable way of working and puts less strain on the frame.

tapestry beater

The chain

When you have warped the requisite number of threads, put down the chain (plait) to regulate the distance between the warp threads. The chain is often made out of double carpet weave 12/6. Start by attaching the yarn round one of the long side ribs $\frac{3}{4}$ in. (2 cm.) from the shorter side rib, and then crochet the warp threads two and two together. (See the illustration on p. 9.) You should use a crochet hook for this. Attach the chain to the opposite side rib and hold the chain firmly and evenly. Instead of crocheting you can use a frame reed, as shown in the illustration on p. 8: let the warp threads run through the empty dents during the warping and at the same time stabilize the density and the width of the warp.

Pattern making

Elisabeth Hoppe

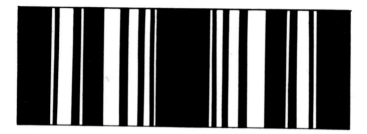

People who have never created their own designs before and who have always relied on instructions and ready-made patterns are often alarmed at the idea and do not think themselves capable of producing satisfactory work, but in the long run you will get much more satisfaction out of making your own designs rather than copying. Skilled instruction is advisable, however, especially if the students concerned are beginners in designing and using colour. We describe below some ways of making patterns independently and try to show you how to develop confidence in the use of colour.

You are sitting down, pencil in hand, determined to create a design. We all have obstacles to overcome, and some people feel that the problems of creation are insurmountable, but everyone should be able to create something concrete. What? Anyone can create pattern pieces, elements of design, so that they form a unified composition. Let's start with what must be the most simple pattern, stripes, which are suitable for the warp of a scarf or a dress fabric, for example, and let's plan to make it in such a way that the colours of the warp will not affect the weft. Using black paper, cut out a number of strips of equal width. Lay them on white paper so that the white gaps are as wide as the black strips. (See the illustration on p. 27, above.) We have now made a striped pattern, but this pattern is not very interesting, because all we have done is to establish rules which give no scope for variations.

All the pattern pieces are equal in width, as are the gaps, and since we are going to have a warp, the direction of the stripe is predetermined. The difference in tone between black and white is so great and the edges between them so clear-cut that the pattern seems to 'clash'.

Now cut some very narrow strips of black paper and place them on either side of the wide ones. The pattern will become less monotonous as soon as you have stripes and gaps of different widths. The narrow stripes complement the black and white areas so that the pattern no longer clashes.

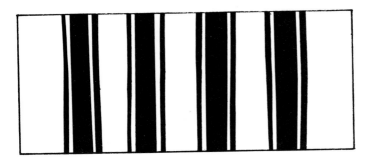

Now replace every other group of stripes with a group of three or five narrow stripes. Although you still have only two different widths, you have varied the pattern by placing the lines closer together.

Managing to keep the pattern pieces close together is one of the more important factors in pattern-making. (It is much easier to cut out pattern pieces in paper and move them around until you are satisfied than to draw and rub out endlessly.)

(Left) The stripes become narrower while the gaps between them remain the same. (Right) Stripes and gaps become narrower.

The stripes become thinner, the gaps remaining the same, followed by a repetition of the entire design.

Stripes of different widths arranged in groups with an equal distance between them.

The same striped pattern, with black and white reversed.

The striped pattern above illustrates the yarn windings on pp. 30, 35, and 36.

We have now approached what may be called the dynamics of configuration, general impression and relationships. The relationship between the colour and shape of a pattern and its background is the foundation of designing. Cut out stripes of different widths, several of each width, and arrange them according to your own rules, symmetrically or asymmetrically, until you have an attractive pattern. (See the illustrations on this page.)

You will soon realize why certain rules are necessary; without them, you might just as well scatter the pattern pieces at random, which results in chaos rather than a design. But too many rules may give rise to the sort of effect shown in the first example, where no room is left for your own imagination. You will most probably find that something in between these two extremes gives the most satisfying results. These remarks about rules for design apply equally to rules for the use of colour.

In order to illustrate the importance of the properties of colour in design, we started with warping in black and white, after which we have transferred the pattern into two shades of grey.

Most of the grey hues have been arranged in a different order so that you can hardly tell that the two examples come from the same basic pattern. In pattern A we have four narrow stripes of one hue of light grey laid between stripes of another hue of light grey. These colours are so similar in tone that the narrow stripes almost disappear. In pattern B we have used a hue of dark grey for the narrow stripes, arranged between a light grey and white, so that the dark stripes stand out strongly, giving character to the design. The four fairly narrow stripes of medium grey are the only ones which have been placed identically in both patterns. From these examples you can see that tones have a very important effect on the look of the pattern. Before we go any further and use colour in patterns A and B, we must examine the other properties of colour — tone and strength.

(Below) Top. Yarn windings in black and white, putting into practice the exercise in cutting out on page 29. A. The same design, wound with grey yarns. B. The grey yarns placed in a different order.

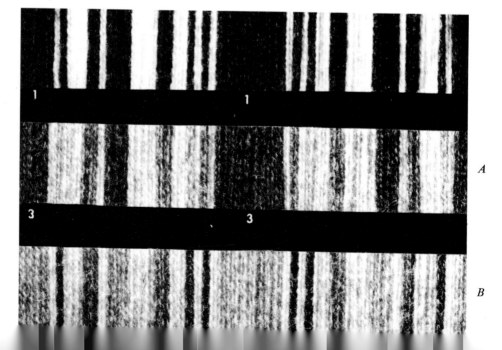

Colour

Elisabeth Hoppe

Speaking the same language

When people try to describe colour to each other it soon be-
comes clear that no one speaks the same language. You may
perhaps describe colour by using analogies (for example,
lemon-yellow, sky-blue, and so on), but it is not possible to
achieve any degree of accuracy in this way, as the colour of
lemons differs according to their ripeness and the colour of the
sky is different on a cold autumn day from that on a hot summer
one. At the moment 'plum' is a popular way of describing a
colour which can mean almost anything except yellow and
green. Another way of describing colours is by the impression
they give — greeny-yellow, for example — and by the use of an
auxiliary word such as pale, light, dark, strong, and so on. In
this way the actual impression of colour can be systematized.
Such a system has been worked out by Ewald Hering, a German
scientist, who calls it the natural colour system.

This system is quite reasonable, since it makes use of our own
observations of the differing properties of colour. No atlas, no
scientific instrument for measuring the radiation or wavelength
of light, is needed to compare the impression or appearance of
colour. In the 1920s Tryggve Johannson, a physicist with an
immense interest in art and design, realized that Hering's
method could be developed into an even more precise system.
This was done by dividing the properties of colour into (1) hue,
(2) light and (3) strength, and arranging these on a colour
chart with black, white, red, blue, and green as fixed points.

You will see by looking at a rainbow or at light breaking
through a prism that colours always come in the same order —
red, orange, yellow, green, blue, and violet. Try to imagine a
section of a rainbow bent into a circle, with the red on the right,
the yellow on top, the green to the left, and the blue below. We
experience these four colours as pure and unmixed, and we call
them foundation colours; together with black and white they
make up the elementary colours. Note that we are talking about
the impression which colours give; although green is made from
yellow and blue and could therefore be classed as a secondary
colour, we experience it as an independent colour and not as a
blue-yellow, while we see orange as a yellow-red and violet as

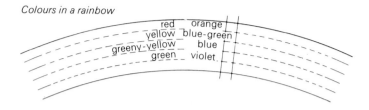

Colours in a rainbow

red orange
yellow blue-green
greeny-yellow blue
green violet.

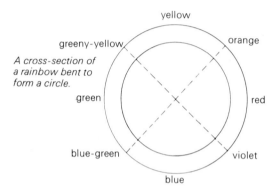

yellow

greeny-yellow orange

*A cross-section of
a rainbow bent to
form a circle.*

green red

blue-green violet

blue

a red-blue. In our circle the shade of orange which appears to be equally yellow and red is placed between the yellow and red, and such colours are called 'mid-colours'. Straight lines are drawn between the foundation colours, dividing the circle into four quadrants; these can now be divided by lines from mid-colour to mid-colour.

This gives segments which are called octants. If you want to describe a colour indicate its position on the colour circle. A colour in the first quadrant is orange; a colour in the first octant of the first quadrant is a yellowish-orange. Colours in the same quadrant are called 'unity' colours; colours next to each other are called 'akimbo' colours, and those in opposite quadrants 'counter' colours. The circle can also be divided into areas of foundation colours; for example, the area from orange to violet is predominantly red. The same applies to the area of the green foundation colours; the area from blue-green to greeny-yellow is predominantly green. If you want to distinguish between the characteristic properties of certain colours, place them on the colour circle. You will find that several different colours appear to

32

have the same hue, that is, they are made up of the same proportion of yellow and red; they will therefore appear in the same position on the colour circle. To decide how they differ, place them in a cross-section of a colour. On the left side make a scale with black at the top and white at the bottom. Place your colour beside a grey of equivalent tone. You will then find that colours differ by another property, strength. Colours which are mostly grey and only faintly tinted are placed near grey shades, whereas brighter ones are placed farther out on the right. At the end furthest from the grey shades you will find the brightest colours, the peak or maximal colours.

Colour Combinations

By adopting a system for describing the properties of colour you can describe them clearly without confusing them. But how can you go on to describe colour combinations? Is it possible to describe the relationships, the links and the tensions between different colours? Many theorists have tried to establish rules for combining colours according to principles of colour harmony. The results have always been rather unsatisfactory, since they have attempted to determine aesthetic perception by their own subjective judgements.

Tryggve Johansson claims that 'A theory should not tie the artist to any particular aesthetic direction, but should give him the freedom to express his knowledge.' Nonetheless, it is probably necessary to use a colour theory to develop the *possibilities* of colour combinations.

Tryggve Johansson's research into colour theories has led to an objective theory of composition. Ready-made formulae for 'beautiful' colour combinations can be derived from this theory, as well as several alternatives relating to changes in colour and composition.

How colours influence each other

You will soon find that colours change and influence each other differently in different combinations. A light-toned colour looks bright against a dark background because it appears to have a higher content of white. The same colour will look duller against a white background because it appears to have a higher content of black. This type of effect is called the 'induction' of

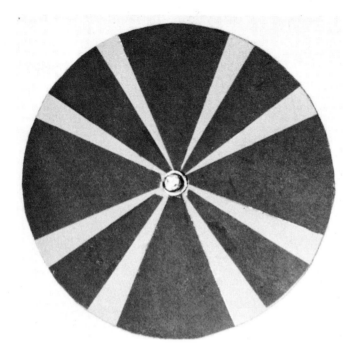

Colour wheel. Cut out pieces of yellow and blue paper. Glue them on to a piece of round card. Put a pin through the centre and allow the wheel to revolve so that the colours seem to blend.

light. (See the illustration.) A pale-coloured object will be similarly affected by a strong-coloured background, and will look even less colourful. If you put a clear yellow against a green background it looks orangey, while on a red background it will look greeny-yellow.

Red and green (complementary colours) contrast with each other in the same way as black and white, dark and light, big and small. Some features of an object placed against one background (tone, lightness, strength of colour, and size) will seem different when the same object is placed against a different background. Complementary colours make each other stand out, whereas when they are mixed they neutralize each other; for instance, a mixture of red and green looks muddy. Make your own experiments by placing pieces of a given colour and shape against different backgrounds and seeing what happens.

If you want to see how colours mix, make a colour wheel. (See the illustration above.)

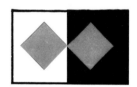

Induction of light.

B (Above). The grey hues with one colour. (Above centre) Mid-colours from the third quadrant with a counter-colour to provide accent. (Below) Several hues of one colour.

A (Above) Colours from one quadrant. (Above centre) Colours from quadrants next to the one above. (Below centre) Colours from opposite quadrants. (Below) Colours from three quadrants.

(Above) The area of the yellow foundation colour. (Above centre) The area of the red foundation colour. (Below centre) The area of the blue foundation colour. (Below) The area of the green foundation colour.

(Above) Composition of two foundation colours, predominantly strong in tone. (Centre) Composition of two foundation colours, predominantly faint in tone. (Below) Colours from the four quadrants. The colours go together because they are all similar in strength and tone, but the pattern doesn't stand out very well.

Analysis of colour transposition

Another method of classifying colours according to their properties is the following: the colour hue is selected as before,
according to the wheel of colour hues. The other properties of
colours are analyzed and marked on a triangle (instead of a
cross-section of colour). The angles of an equilateral triangle
indicate the highest degree of the basic properties — i.e. lightness, darkness, and strength.

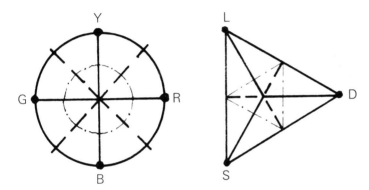

Diagram of colour analysis.

The less white a colour appears to contain, the further away
it is placed from the angle L. A strong colour is placed between
L and D, near to angle D, and if it is dark rather than bright it is
placed near to angle S. Colours in the same area which have
been analyzed in this way are called corresponding colours.
They have the same properties except for the colour itself; i.e. a
green looks as strong as a corresponding red. A good example
of transposition is to interchange corresponding colours from
one colour shade to another.

Colouring — rules of colour

You cannot always work out the colouring of a design by sheer intuition. In order to avoid mistakes it is advisable to work systematically. You can start with simple schemes and then go on to more complicated ones. Start by using pattern B on p. 30. First decide on a simple colour scheme, keeping the three grey shades and the white. Now replace the light grey with a stronger shade of the same colour. Vary it further, by replacing the other greys with reds of an equivalent tone.

The next scheme can be created by replacing all four greys with equivalent greeny-blues. Keep the white, which has no equivalent colour. Vary the scheme by changing to another colour hue. (See pattern B3 on p. 35.)

A third scheme can be produced by replacing three of the greys with colours of equal tone from the first octant in the quadrant. The fourth grey is replaced by a colour with the same light tone from the opposite quadrant, orange. The white stripes remain. (See pattern B2 on p. 35.)

Four different colour combinations of pattern A (p. 30) are shown on p. 35. In all four the dark green is the same, but it is affected by the colours next to it, so that it looks different in each pattern. The narrow grey-green stripes, of which there are four in each pattern, are all the same. So we can see how this neutral-grey is influenced by its background. In the first pattern, colours from the green-yellow quadrant become fainter beside the strong colour. The light greeny-yellow surrounding it makes the dark green appear darker and less colourful. (See pattern A1 on p. 35.) In the other pattern, where other colours are taken from the orange quadrant, the greeny-yellow looks greener. (See pattern A2 on p. 35.) In the fourth pattern the greeny-yellow colours look far more yellow beside the colours from the green-blue quadrant. (See pattern A4 on p. 35.)

Always notice how colours are changed by the influence ('induction') of the colours near them.

We have used pattern B on p. 30 for the four patterns shown above on p. 36. The white stripes remain as they are, whereas the greys have been replaced by the nearest equivalent tone from each area of the foundation colours.

Weaving techniques with variations

Estine Östlund

Those of us who are responsible for the examples of weaving in this book do not mind sharing our experience with others. You are welcome to use our patterns and materials, provided you do not do so commercially. Naturally we hope that you will use the book mainly as a source of inspiration. You will soon find that this is the best way to get real satisfaction from creating with a loom and frame.

Cottolin Weaves

The first weaving instruction in this section relates to the chapter about striped patterns and will show you how to weave with a striped warp without letting the stripes disappear. This can easily happen if you use the wrong quality of yarn or the wrong density of reed.

We start with a cottolin weave for a table runner or table mat. This fabric can be washed easily, and is therefore suitable for modern textiles. If you are planning to have a linen cupboard full of easy-care textiles, cottolin is a good choice. After a couple of washings you no longer need to iron it, you can simply hang it out to dry. Where cottolin is not available, substitute cotton.

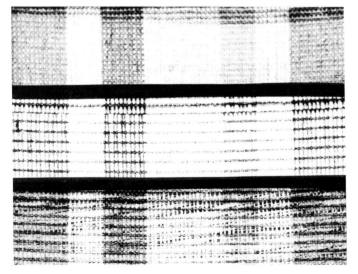

The weft yarn, influenced by the use of colours. (Above) Weft in a medium light tone. It does not influence the warp very much. (Centre) Weft in a very light tone. The stripes are lighter in tone and do not show as in the first example. (Below) Weft in a fairly dark tone, which influences the lighter parts very strongly, with the result that the stripes don't show up properly.

Table runner or table mat

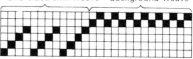

Warp: Coloured cottolin 22/2.
Weft: Every other weft-shot coloured cottolin 22/2. Every other weft-shot string yarn or three-ply coloured candlewick yarn 2/2.
Reed: 50/10*, 1 thread in leash and 2 threads in dent. Selvedge is threaded twice with 3 threads in 2 dents.
Width of reed: 3·2 cm. (about 1¼ in.) for the table runner, 4 cm. (about 1½ in.) for the table mat.
Number of threads: 320 + 4 selvedge threads = 324 threads for the table runner, 400 threads + 4 selvedge threads = 404 threads for the table mat.

Remember that cottolin weaves shrink when they are washed. They shrink 15% in the direction of the warp and 10% in the direction of the weft.

**All reed settings are metric.*

Striped table runner

One-sided twill weave   Leashing on a two-shaft background weave

Warp: Finnish linen yarn 4.
Weft: Finnish linen yarn 4.
Reed: 40/10, 1 thread in leash, 2 threads in each dent for a two-shaft background weave. 1 thread in reed, 3 threads in dent to the twill teeth.

The number of threads in the weave depends upon the width of the stripes. When you calculate the number of threads in this weave, remember that a two-shaft background weave has 8 threads per cm. (about ⅜ in.), whereas the twill teeth have 12 threads per cm.

Striped fabric in a one-sided twill weave on a two-shaft background weave.

'Panama' cloth ('Hopsack').

Warp: Coloured cottolin 22/2.
Weft: Linen yarn 4 U.K.
Reed: 45/10, 1 thread in leash and 2 threads in dent. The selvedge is threaded twice with 3 threads in dent.
Width of reed: 9 cm. (about 3⅜ in.).
Number of threads: 810 threads + 4 selvedge threads = 814 threads.
Number of weft-shots: 9 (of a 2-ply yarn) per 2 cm. (about ¾ in.).

If you want a coarser weave you must weave with two yarns (or alternatively, with a thicker yarn). You will then be faced with the problem of how to retain the striped pattern, as the warp and the weft affect the finished result. The stripes will not stand out as well if the weave is coarser.

In this example we have used the principle known as colour mixing to overcome this problem. We selected pale colours for the warp and strong colours for the weft. Although the structure is coarser, we have managed to maintain the colour strength and the relationship between the different hues of the warp colours. This fabric is used particularly for furnishings, spring coats, trousers, and perhaps a bathrobe and towel. This type of fabric can also be used for a long skirt.

Furnishing fabric in a one-way herring-bone weave

Warp: Cottolin 22/2.
Weft: Linen yarn 4 U.K.
Reed: 60/10, 1 thread in leash and 1 thread in dent.
Number of weft-shots: 10 per cm. (about ⅜ in.).

A furnishing fabric with a one-way twill weave is always woven to wear in the warp rather than the weft direction. To achieve the maximum wear always upholster a piece of furniture so that the stripes will run from the back to the front, never across the seat.

Linen is recommended for a piece of furniture which is well padded, since you do not need to consider the elasticity of the weave. We suggest a heavy weight for a furnishing fabric. It is then strong enough for decorating a teenager's room, a country cottage, or a log hut. You can also use it for making handbags. (See the colour illustration on p. 53.) As we have already said, cottolin shrinks more than linen, so don't forget to allow for this when you are calculating the warp.

Woollen weaves

We have already explained how to keep the stripes in a cottolin weave, which is obviously equally applicable to cotton and linen individually. But woollen weaves behave differently. Fluffy woollen yarns can alter the general effect created by colours in a weave, for instance, if a red warp is used with a green weft. They are both elementary colours and therefore modify each other's colour strength. The general impression of colour is reduced, resulting in a brownish effect.

You must always keep an eye open for colour mixtures. If you want to keep a clear and distinct warp stripe you must choose a weft that harmonizes with the warp.

Wool must undergo various finishing processes, which you can carry out yourself only on a few types of wool. Most fabrics will have to be sent out to a professional finisher. (See p. 23 for further information on this point.)

Dress fabric

A lightweight dress fabric is the most popular type of material. Hand-woven fabrics are comfortable to wear, since they 'breathe' and are crease-resistant and flexible.

Warp: Coloured botany wool 20/2 and tapestry yarn.
Weft: Coloured botany wool 20/2.
Reed: 80/10, 1 thread in leash, 1 thread in dent.
Width of reed: 9 cm. (about $3\frac{3}{8}$ in.).
Number of threads: 720 threads + 4 selvedge threads = 724 threads.
Number of weft-shots: 11 per 2 cm. (about $\frac{3}{4}$ in.).
Finishing process: Send away for finishing. (Give information about what the fabric is to be used for.)

42

The relationship between the colours is reversed in this example compared with the 'panama' cloth on p. 41. In the other example we used a subdued warp and a colourful weft. In this example we have used a strongly coloured warp, which is modified by a lighter-coloured weft. (See the colour illustration on p. 53.)

A long skirt

What about wearing a long skirt instead of trousers? Long skirts are feminine, flattering and easily adaptable to different occasions. For instance, a sweater and a leather belt makes the skirt suitable for a cosy evening at home, whereas a slinky blouse with bishop sleeves makes it appropriate for smarter occasions. The leather belt can be replaced by an elegant belt woven by the weft-picked 'crab's nest' technique. The belt can be lined with a smart silk lining. (See the colour illustration on p. 56.)

Warp: 2 ply Shetland.
Weft: 2 ply Shetland.
Reed: 50/10, 1 thread in leash and 1 thread in dent.
Number of weft-shots: 5 per cm. (about $\frac{3}{8}$ in.).
Finishing process: Send away for finishing. (Give information about what the fabric is to be used for.)

A twill-weave fabric for coats, suits, and skirts

Close-up of twill weave fabric for coats, suits, and skirts.

By means of continuous leashings on four shafts and a yarn suitable for furnishing fabric 6/1 in the warp, you can produce different weaves for coat, suit, or skirt fabrics. The idea is to vary the knotting and the thickness of the weft yarn.

Warp: 5 cut Cheviot wool.
Weft: 1 thread 11 cut Cheviot wool in every other weft-shot, and 2 threads 5 cut Cheviot wool for furnishing fabric 6/1 and 1 thread linen 16/1 twisted together for every other weft-shot.
Reed: 55/10, 1 thread in leash, 1 thread in dent.
Width of reed: 9 cm. (about $3\frac{3}{8}$ in.).
Number of threads: 495 + 4 selvedge threads = 499 threads.
Finishing process: Send away to be finished. (Give information about what the fabric is to be used for.)

with levers   without levers

See also the suggestions for weaves under the heading 'Variations on a rose path theme' on p. 57.

Scarf in two-shaft plain weave

Warp: Alpaca/wool.
Weft: Alpaca/wool.
Reed: 40/10, 1 thread in leash and 1 thread in dent.
Width of reed: 2·8 cm. (about $1\frac{1}{4}$ in.).
Number of threads: 112 + 4 selvedge threads = 116 threads.
Weft-shots: 8–9 shots per 2 cm. (about $\frac{3}{4}$ in.).
Finishing process: Send away to be finished. (Give information about the finished width required.)

An Alpaca and wool mixture makes an excellent material for scarves. Ideally it should consist of 40% wool and 60% Alpaca wool. This mixture of different fibre yarns produces a very soft fabric. Alpaca does not absorb dye very well, so the wool is dyed separately and then interspun with non-bleached alpaca. (See the colour illustration on p. 53.)

A scarf in a twill weave fabric

with levers   without levers

Warp: 3 ply knitting wool.
Weft: Botany wool 10/2.
Reed: 45/10, 1 thread in reed and 1 thread in dent.
Width of reed: 2·8 cm. (about $1\frac{1}{4}$ in.).
Number of threads: 126 + 4 selvedge threads = 130 threads.
Number of weft-shots: 8–9 per 2 cm. (about $\frac{3}{4}$ in.)

44

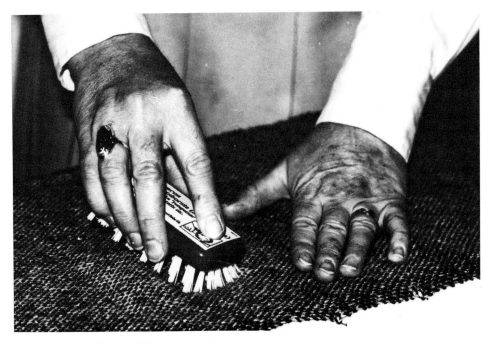

Finishing a scarf. The wool fibres are brushed up.

Finishing process: one of the differences between the scarf made out of wool and Alpaca and one made out of knitting yarn is that you can finish the latter yourself. This is done by dipping the weave into lukewarm water (approx. 95 °F. or 35 °C.), and then squeezing out the water. Now lay the weave on something flat like an ironing board and attach it with drawing pins or ordinary pins. Finally, brush and raise the wool fibres in the warp and weft directions with a medium-hard brush.

Shawl

Warp: Botany wool 2/10.
Weft: Mohair (70 yds. per oz.)
Reed: 40/10, 1 thread in leash and 1 thread in dent.
Width of reed: 6 cm. (about 2⅜ in.)
Number of threads: 240 + 4 selvedge threads = 244 threads.
Weft-shots: 9 per 2 cm. (about ¾ in.)
Finishing process: As above.

A similar weave to the scarf weave is obtained by the shawl and plaid weaves. Follow the same directions, but use a denser reed. This does not mean that you pick a thicker reed, but that you use something like 30/10 with 1 thread in the leash and 2 threads in the dent.

Plaid

Warp: Homespun 2/17 cut.
Weft: Homespun 2/17 cut.
Reed: 30/10, 1 thread in leash and 2 threads in dent.
Width of reed: 14 cm. (about $5\frac{1}{4}$ in.)
Number of threads: 840 + 4 selvedge threads = 844 threads.
Weft-shots: 5–6 per cm. (about $\frac{3}{8}$ in.)
Finishing process: Send away to be finished as a plaid.

with levers

without levers

Double weave on a small loom

A small loom with a 60–90 cm. (about $22\frac{1}{2}$–$33\frac{3}{4}$ in.) weave is not wide enough for weaving plaids. One way of solving this problem is to weave twice as long a weave and join the weaves selvedge to selvedge before they are finished. It is difficult to obtain two weaves exactly the same length, so that the fringes correspond in length, but this problem can be overcome by weaving two layers of cloth at the same time, leaving the right selvedge open and interweaving the left one. The weave is folded in the loom. We suggest the following method:

Warp: Done with 2 threads.
Spreading: 1 group = 4 threads threaded into every other dent.
Leashing: continuously on four shafts.
Reeding: 1 thread from the first shaft and 1 thread from the second shaft are threaded into 1 reed. 1 thread from the third shaft is threaded into the second reed with 1 thread from the fourth shaft. During the leashing process you leave every other dent empty on the left-hand side at the two protruding pairs of threads. This is done to avoid a denser stripe in the centre of the weave. The fringe can be either twisted or plaited.

46

A double-woven plaid for children

You can weave a child's plaid in a loom that is only 60 cm. (about 22½ in.) wide. If you use the method suggested above you can still obtain a weave 120 cm. (about 45 in.) wide without joining.

with levers   without levers

Warp: Botany wool 10/2.
Weft: Mohair (70 yds. per oz.).
Reed: 50/10, 1 thread in leash, 2 threads in dent.
Width of reed: 6 cm. (about 2¼ in.)
Number of threads: 600.
Finishing process: Send away for plaid finishing.

A double-woven poncho

You can weave a poncho in the same way. (See the coloured illustration on p. 53.)

Warp: 4 ply knitting wool.
Weft: 4 ply knitting wool.
Reed: 40/10, 1 thread in leash, 2 threads in dent.
Width of reed: 5·6 cm. (about 2½ in.)
Number of threads: 223 × 2 = 446 threads.
Weft-shots: 8–9 per 2 cm (about ¾ in.)
Leashing card: See children's plaid.
We have allowed 1·5 cm. (about ½ in.) + fringe of 1 cm. (about ⅜ in.) for the collar. The illustration on p. 48 shows you how to fringe.

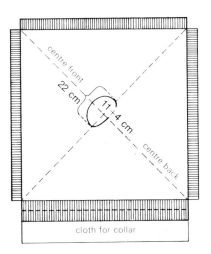

A diagram for cutting out a poncho with collar.

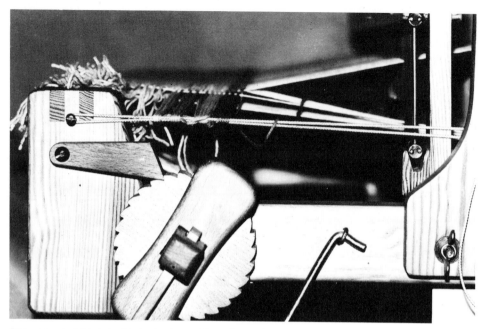

The weave is folded double in the loom. Tie and stretch a piece of string along the right-hand side of the loom and let the weft-shots pass round it each time so as to have an even fringe all round. (See pp. 55-56.)

One warp — many weaves

The preparation is the most time-consuming part of the whole weaving process. Warping, spreading, pulling on, leashing sleying, knotting, top-tying, and under-tying — it all takes time.

To avoid repeating the preparation process for each different weave, a basic warp may be set up which can be used for different types of weave. The following instructions explain how you can set up a basic warp.

You can weave mats on to a two-shaft background weave using narrow strips of rug (5–7 cm. or 2–2¾ in.). The warp is also suitable for a tapestry weave using the *röllakan*, 'Russian', or *snärj* ('entangled') methods. In using this warp you can also play around on the diagonal in a 'crab's nest' pattern and make free interpretations of many techniques.

Basic warp

Warp: Unbleached linen yarn 16/3.
Reed: 35/10, 1 thread in leash, 1 thread in dent.
Width of reed: 4·2 cm. (about 1⅝ in.)
Number of threads: 148 + 4 selvedge threads = 152 threads.
The hem of the mats is woven out of linen yarn 16/2 or cottolin 22/2.
Weft for röllakan: 2/2½s worsted tapestry yarn.
Weft for 'Russian' weave: 2-ply wool yarn for the foundation, linen or wool yarns for the pattern.
Weft for snärj weave: 1 thread unbleached linen + 1 thread linen 16/2 plyed together for the foundation, wool or linen yarns for the pattern.
Weft for 'crab's nest': Same as for the *snärj* weave.

A	B with levers	C without levers

A. Mat weave
   Röllakan

Snärj weave

'Crab's nest'

B. Russian weave

C. Russian weave

Playing with super ellipses. Technique: soumak, which is a variation of the snärj *technique. Designed and woven by Estine Ostlund.*

Lace-up boot. Tapestry weave in röllakan. Assessment work by May Engman.

Monk's belt

'Monk's belt' is an attractive weaving technique by which you can make up your own fairly free patterns. We leashed just one star of monk's belt and then made up the rest of the design in the actual loom.

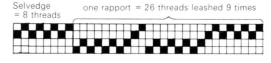

Warp: 2/2½s worsted tapestry yarn.
Basic weft: 2/2½s worsted tapestry yarn.
Weft-picks for the pattern: Woollen yarns and lurex.
Reed: 50/10, 1 thread in leash, 1 thread in dent.
Width of reed: 4·8 cm. (about 1⅞ in.)
Number of threads: 242 + 2 selvedge threads = 244 threads.
Number of weft-shots: 5 per cm. (about ⅜ in.)

50

The MMF technique

The MMF technique (invented by Märta Måås-Fjetterström) is a simplified version of the *röllakan* technique in which the two-shaft weft yarns and the weft yarn for the pattern are shot through one after another into the same shed. The MMF technique is a more open weave suitable for lampshades or for window curtains.

Decorations for windows and French windows (I)

Warp: Semi-bleached linen yarn 16/1.
Weft: Semi-bleached linen yarn 8 for the foundation, coloured wool or linen yarn for the pattern.
Reed: 50/10, 2 threads in leash, 2 threads in dent.
Number of weft-shots: 5 per cm. (about $\frac{3}{8}$ in.)

'Spring'. A window-shade woven by the MMF technique. The cover is intended to be fitted over French windows. Designed and woven by Elisabeth Hoppe.

Decorations for windows and French windows (II)

Warp: Semi-bleached linen yarn 8.
Weft: Semi-bleached linen yarn 6 for the foundation, coloured wool and linen yarns for the pattern.
Reed: 50/10, 1 thread in leash, 1 thread in dent.
Number of weft-shots: 5 per cm. (about $\frac{3}{8}$ in.)

Suggestion for a curtain

The MMF technique can create a most attractive effect on a curtain, but it is important to choose a softer yarn than for the other examples of the MMF technique.

Warp: Semi-bleached linen yarn 12.
Weft: Linen yarn 16/2.
Reed: 55/10, 1 thread in leash, 1 thread in dent.
Number of weft-shots: 5–6 per cm. (about $\frac{3}{8}$ in.)
Pattern yarn: Coloured linen 16/2 or yarn used for furnishing fabrics 6/1, and coloured linen 16/1.

An original use of the MMF technique. Circle on a two-shaft background weave decorated with geometric shapes. Designed and woven by Maija Kolsi-Mäkelä.

Tablecloth woven in a frame by the MMF technique. The white shapes are woven out of strips cut from cotton-lawn rugs. Designed and woven by Rita Lundberg.

(Above) Strong furnishing fabric in a reversible twill weave. (For instructions see p. 41.) (Below) A thin yellow dress fabric on a two-shaft background weave. (See p. 42.) 'Panama' cloth. (For instructions see p. 41.)
(Above) Cap and scarf. (For instructions see p. 44.) (Below) A poncho. (For instructions and pattern see p. 47.)

(Above) 'Spring in March', a nature study. Tapestry weave in a frame. Designed and woven by Rut Holm. (Below left) 'Tree', a nature study. Woven according to the MMF technique. (See also p. 51.) Designed and woven by Karin Edenfeldt. (Below right) 'Beach pebbles', a nature study. Executed according to the tapestry technique. Designed and woven by Rita Lundberg. (Opposite) Tapestry weave in a frame. The castle is decorated with curled shavings. Designed and woven by Rita Lundberg.

(Left) 'The Church of Amål', a free
interpretation of a monk's belt. (See also p. 50.)
Assessment work by Alice Krusenblad. (Above)
Free interpretation of peonies. A curtain woven by
means of the MMF technique. (See also p. 51.)
Designed and woven by Elisabeth Hoppe. (Below)
'Crab's nest', weft-picked at random. A pattern
suggestion for a belt. (See the long skirt on p. 43.)

Variations on a 'rose path' theme

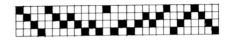

A linen curtain

Warp: Unbleached linen yarn 12.
Weft: Semi-bleached linen yarn 8.
Reed: 70/10, 1 thread in leash, 1 thread in dent.
Width of reed: 10 cm. (about 3¾ in.)
Number of threads: 700 + 4 selvedge threads = 704 threads.
Number of weft-shots: 6–7 per cm. (about ⅜ in.)

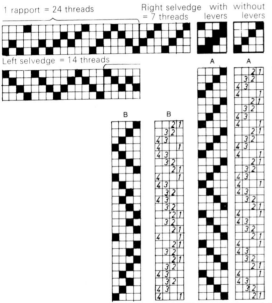

A and B are two different pattern variations.

A linen table runner

Warp: Linen yarn 6.
Weft: Linen yarn 6.
Reed: 50/10, 1 thread in leash, 2 threads in dent.
Width of reed: 1·8 cm. (about 11/16 in.)
Number of threads: 189 + 4 selvedge threads = 193 threads.

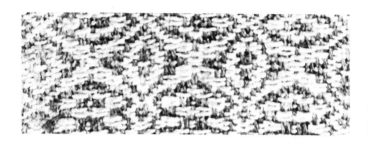

Detail of a linen table runner, woven according to pedal card B.

Fabric for coats, suits, and skirts

Warp: 16 cut Cheviot wool.
Weft: 2/17 cut homespun wool.
Reed: 50/10, 1 thread in leash, 1 thread in dent.
Number of threads: 450 + 4 selvedge threads = 454 threads.
Number of weft-shots: 9–10 per 2 cm. (about $\frac{3}{4}$ in.)
Finishing process: Send away for finishing. (Give information about what the material is to be used for.)

Detail of skirt, suit, and coat fabric. The handbag on p. 76 is woven by following these instructions.

Wall-hanging in brown and white. It is hung from the rail by brown suede loops.

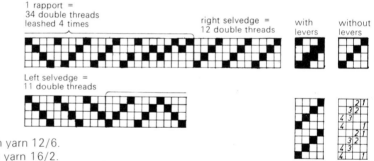

1 rapport =
34 double threads
leashed 4 times

right selvedge =
12 double threads

with levers

without levers

Left selvedge =
11 double threads

Wall-hanging

Warp: Coloured cotton yarn 12/6.
Weft: Coloured cotton yarn 16/2.
Reed: 25/10, 2 threads in leash and 2 threads in dent.
Width of reed: 5 cm. (about 1⅞ in.)
Number of threads: 250 + 4 selvedge threads = 254 threads.

We wove a tapestry weave, using the same basic weave. It is interesting to see how this technique, a variation on the 'rose path' technique, plays an important part in the finished design. (See the colour illustration on p. 17.)

Weft-picked damask

Damask is a very difficult technique which was very popular in the eighteenth century, but has since been almost forgotten. We want to help revive it by showing you a variation known as 'weft-picked damask'. This variation can be woven without either pattern pulling or pattern harness, which are normally always associated with weaving damask. We do want to stress that beginners will not be able to manage this technique, but experienced weavers can adopt it if they follow the detailed instructions given below.

Warp: 2 hues of coloured linen yarn 16/2.
Weft: 1 thread coloured linen yarn 16/1, 1 thread lurex, 1 thread coloured linen yarn 16/2 plyed together with 1 thread coloured linen yarn 16/1.
Reed: 40/10, 1 thread in leash, 2 threads in dent.

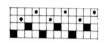

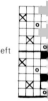

⊡ = light warp thread

■ = dark warp thread

⊠ = pattern thread in the weft

■ = thin weft thread

⊡ = Lurex weft

Method:

Warp with threads of linen yarn 16/2 in similar shades, one lighter and the other darker in tone. Leash according to leash cards 1, 3, 2, 4, putting the lighter threads on to the first and second shafts and the darker threads on to the third and fourth shafts. The weave is shuttled three times: twice for the two-shaft weft-shots, and once for the weft-shots for the pattern. We used a very thin thread of linen 16/1 on one shuttle and a simple lurex thread on the other for the two-shaft weft-shots. It is advisable to select one light and one dark hue for the weft-shots for the pattern, perhaps in contrasting colours, so that the pattern will stand out as clearly as possible. We decided to ply 1 thread of linen 16/2 and 1 thread of linen 16/1 together for our weft-shots. But you can weave just about any pattern you want.

Draw the pattern on graph paper and then calculate how many threads will correspond to one square. You can also draw the pattern actual size and attach it under the warp. First weave a little piece according to the pedal card, but without any weft-shots. You can start by weaving a couple of simple squares to make sure that you understand the technique.

Weft-picks for the pattern: Lower pedal 1, and pick up the lowered threads from underneath with pick-up sticks, so that the threads that will produce the pattern are tied underneath the pick-up sticks. Lower pedal 4 and shoot through the pattern thread. Pull out the pick-up sticks and beat the weave with the beater. Continue with two-shaft shots and a weft-shot for the pattern on pedal 3, just as you have done with the previous pedal. This pattern is tied in a similar way to the 'Russian' weave.

Double-weaves

Double-weaves with patterns (both reversible and one-sided double-weaves) are often called Finnish weaves, although this is not a very good name, since they are known as splintered weaves in Finland! This is exactly what they are: the weave consists of two layers, in which the pattern has been weft-picked by means of splinters and pick-up sticks.

	with levers	without levers

A reversible individual double-weave

The following fabrics are suitable to start with until you get to know the technique better. (See also fabric suggestions on p. 65.)

■ = top warp
× = bottom warp

Warp: Coloured cotton yarn 12/12 for the top weave, unbleached cotton yarn 12/12 for the bottom weave.
Weft: Coloured cotton yarn 12/12 for the top weave, unbleached cotton yarn 12/12 for the bottom weave.
Reed: 45/10, 1 thread in leash, 2 threads in dent.
Both weaves must have the same number of threads and the same length. The pattern (drawn on graph paper) consists of certain squares which must be filled in. 1 square = 2 top threads + 2 bottom threads = 4 threads.

Spreading: One group of threads from the top weave is threaded in to the first dent, one group of threads from the bottom warp is threaded in to the second dent, and so on.

Leashing: Top warp on the first and second shafts, bottom warp on the third and fourth shafts.

Sleying: Two threads, one of each colour, in to each dent. Start by using one thread from the top warp for the first dent, and then one thread for each dent. Then use one thread of each colour (i.e. 2 threads in dent). Finally, one thread from the bottom warp goes into the last dent.

Flat-weaving: Press down the pedals to lower the entire bottom warp. Pull a stick behind the reed through the shed that has formed. Both layers are now separated. Use pedals 1 and 2 to push the weft-shot into the top weave. Use pedals 3 and 4 to push the weft-shot into the bottom weave. Pedal continuously 1,2,3,4, and so on. Finish with two weft-shots through the top weave. Pull out the sticks.

Weft-picking the pattern: This process is illustrated on pp. 63–64. The method given applies to a loom with four shafts. On a loom with six pedals, the fifth and sixth pedals can be used for weft-picking the pattern. Otherwise the method is the same as before.

The pattern for a double-weave must be drawn on graph paper, as in the illustration below. On the left you can see the finished result. (Fabric instructions on p. 65.) Designed and woven by Rut Holm.

Weaving in the bottom warp:

1. Lower pedals 3 and 4. The top warp is raised. Pull a pick-up stick in between the warps and lower the appropriate number of threads according to the instructions.

2. Put the sticks in to the warp horizontally. Transfer the threads behind the reed with stick 2. Remove stick 1, which is in front of the reed.

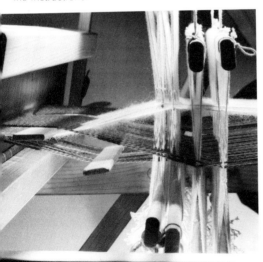

3. Lower pedals 1 and 2. Stick 2 is now locked in the warp. Put stick 1 behind the reed into the shed that has been formed during the last weft-picking.

4. Lower pedal 3, forming a shed in the bottom warp. The first weft is woven by means of the shuttle of the bottom weave. Lower pedal 4 and the second weft is woven.

5. Lower pedals 1 and 2. The bottom warp is raised. Pick up the relevant number of threads with stick 1, and put them into the pattern. (NB: The same number of threads as in the weft-picks on the bottom weave.)

6. Stick 1, is put into the warp horizontally. The threads behind the reed are transferred by means of stick 2. Remove stick 1, which is in front of the reed.

7. Lower pedals 3 and 4. Stick 2 is now locked between the warp. Stick 1 is put into the bottom shed that has been formed during the weft-picking process for the pattern.

8. Lower pedal 1 and a shed is formed in the top warp. The first weft is woven by means of the shuttle of the top weave. Lower pedal 2 and the second weft is woven.

Reversible patterned double-weave — a fabric variation

Warp: 2 threads tapestry yarn for the top weave, unbleached linen yarn 20/3 for the bottom weave.
Weft: 2 threads tapestry yarn plyed together for the top weave, 2-ply linen yarn 20/3 for the bottom weave.
Reed: 50/10, 1 thread in leash, 2 threads in dent.
Number of weft-shots: 5 per cm. (about $\frac{3}{8}$ in.)
Both warps must have the same number of threads and the same length. The wool warp is much more elastic than a linen warp, and must be held more firmly when it is pulled on. It must always be the top warp.

A Viking ship, woven in a frame according to the suggestions above. Designed and woven by Elisabeth Hoppe.

65

*Reversible patterned double-weave in a frame
(drawing by Rita Lundberg)*

Number of weft-shots: 40 per 10 cm. (about 3¾ in.) Warp on 4
nails, leaving the fifth. The distances are regulated by the chain.
Warp and weft: Thick tapestry yarn in both warps, or thick yarn

Weft-picking the pattern of a double-weave in a frame.

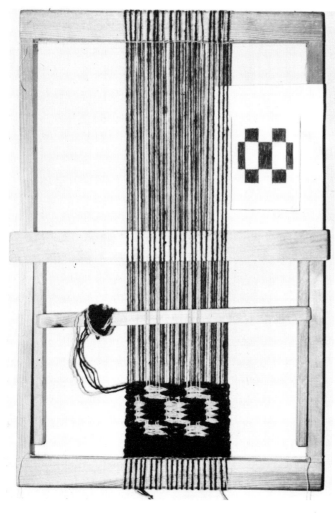

only in the bottom warp. Choose two colours that will make the pattern stand out, such as black and white, brown and white, and so on. Warp both colours at the same time, with one thread more in the top warp. Thread a stick between the two warps. Put a chain into each warp at both ends (= 4 chains). Open the shed at both ends (using thin warp sticks).

Pattern interpretation: The pattern is drawn on graph paper, and woven with the right side facing upwards. 1 horizontal square = 2 threads from both warps. 1 vertical square = 2 weft-shots in to both warps. A flat weave is woven separately in the top and bottom warps. Start and finish in the top warp.

Weaving the pattern: Pick up the pattern (according to the first row of squares on the paper pattern) one and one, on the left side of the bottom threads of the top warp. The bottom warp will move over to the left, leaving one more thread in the top warp, also on the left side. Weave 2 wefts in the bottom warp, with the same yarn as in the warp itself. Now weave 2 wefts in the top warp again with the same yarn as in the top warp. Pick up the next row of patterns and continue in the same sequence.

Variations on a double-weave in a frame

Suggestions for materials and density of the warp: 1. Cowhair yarn or any other coarse yarn. Density of warp: 15/10. 2. Linen yarn. 4. Density of warp: 40/10. 3. Yarn for finishing fabrics, 2 threads. Density of warp: 50/10. The first two alternative weaves are recommended for trying out this technique.

Suggestion for a simplified method of weaving: Use only one warp stick between the layers, and one warp stick for weft-picking the pattern. (See also the weave in the frame on p. 66.)

Once you have grasped the basic principle, you can vary the technique in many ways to create whatever pattern you want. For instance, you can weft-pick the bottom threads two and two between every other top thread, or you can make both edges of the patterns even or jagged.

Ideas for patterns

Elisabeth Hoppe

Cutting out in black and white

1. Cut out a pattern in black paper, unfold it, and glue it on to white paper. When you have obtained a satisfactory pattern, transfer it on to paper and colour it according to the principles described on p. 38.

(Above) Cutting exercise for a handbag. (See p. 76.) Designed and woven by Rita Lundberg.

(Left) Decorative weave based on the cutting illustration next to it. Only the frame and the pattern piece have been woven; the warp threads are left loose in the rest of the weave. This is known as the 'transparent' technique. Designed and woven by Rita Lundberg.

Half of the purse, based on the illustration next to it, is woven in the 'Flemish' fashion. Designed and woven by Rita Lundberg.

2. Cut out a pattern in black paper, unfold it and cut in to the unfolded part, then refold it.

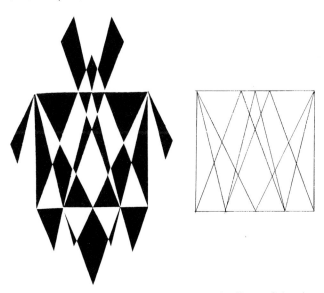

3. Cut out a black square according to the lines of the drawing, and unfold every other piece. Glue it on to white paper.

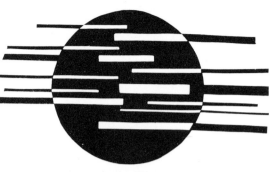

4. Cut straight strips in different widths and lengths. Pull them completely or partly apart. *Variations:* Cut an arc out of a circle

'The moon'. MMF and snärj techniques. Designed and woven by Rut Holm.

70

and pull it apart. If it is transferred to graph paper it can be used as a pattern for an equilateral double-weave.

'Castle'. Tapestry weave based on a complicated cut-out design, with beads sewn on. Designed and woven by Rita Lundberg.

5. Cut out and remove every other piece.

The pattern pieces are placed at irregular intervals, but the picture has a feeling of uniformity because all the pieces are facing in the same direction. The colours are chosen from the same quadrant, which makes the picture hang together. Designed and woven by Rut Holm.

6. Cut out the pieces and arrange them in groups.
Variation: Cut out several simple shapes of different sizes. Arrange them in groups in whatever pattern you fancy.

A cutting exercise is transformed into a pattern

Draw some circles and ellipses with a glass or a cup and cut them out. Put them on to a fairly large piece of paper and experiment with different ways of grouping them. Some people like symmetrical arrangements or borders, while others prefer more asymmetrical patterns. Allow yourself enough time to arrange the pattern pieces, so that you can study them and see whether the design is uniform, and whether the pieces relate properly to each other. If not, what has gone wrong? Are the gaps between the pieces too big? Does the picture seem out of balance because there are too many pieces in one corner, or because the ellipses move in too many different directions? Even with shapes as simple as these you can see how important the distance between the different pieces is for the overall unity of the design. The angle at which they are placed can be used to hold them together or to scatter them. Glue the pattern pieces on to a piece of paper.

We shall now colour them. If you do not feel confident with colours, you can first shade in the pattern with various grey tones and then apply the colour. Take into account the differences in tone from one colour to another so that the pattern really does create whatever effect you want to achieve.

We decided to illustrate this exercise in composition by a simple, stylized motif of fruit, suitable for tapestry weaves. (We don't want to tie you down to this example, however; we want everyone to follow his or her own tastes and to express them. We will mainly use colours from the orange quadrant, but we will select contrasting colours for the leaves from the bluish-green quadrant.

We have already talked about the influence of one colour on another in the chapter about colour (p. 33), so you know that it is best to start by deciding on your background colour. We chose brown for the first two examples. A plain brown background would be very boring both to look at and to weave. In early Flemish weaves the larger areas are divided up by diagonal lines and woven in sections, though it is still all the same colour. The background is divided into fairly large areas. (Note the angles). You can vary the effect by using different shades of brown, but don't make the tones too different, because this can easily make the background too busy, spoiling the actual pattern.

The pieces of fruit must also be divided into segments of different colours or else they will lack dimension and look uninteresting. To make them appear round, you must use light and shading in an appropriate fashion. Imagine that the light comes from the top right-hand corner. The segments numbered 1 in the illustration will therefore be the lightest in tone.

The larger areas are divided by diagonal lines.

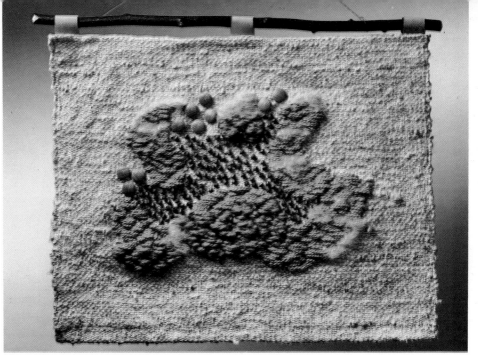

(Above) Wall-hanging. Free interpretation of 'crab's nest'. (For instructions see p. 60.) Assessment work by May Engman.

A storm over snow-clad mountains inspired this tapestry weave designed and woven by Rita Lundberg.

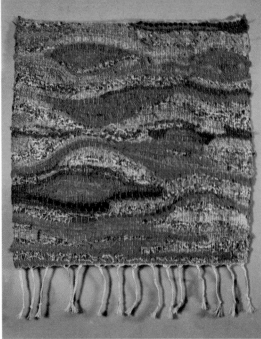

Flemish rug weave. Designed and woven by Viveka Lund (above) and Rut Holm (below).

(Above left) 'The Milky Way'. Glass beads threaded on to the warp and secured by non-spun wool. Designed and woven by Elisabeth Hoppe. (Below left) Lampshade woven very loosely with linen yarn and with weft-picks of non-spun wool. Designed and woven by Birgitta Dahlberg.

(Above right) An oriental town, woven in a frame. The idea underlying the pattern is taken from old hinges. (See also p. 79.) Designed and woven by Estine Östlund. (Below right) 'The Cape of Waldemar', a nature study. A free interpretation of a tapestry weave. (See also p. 83.) Designed and woven by Birgitta Dahlberg.

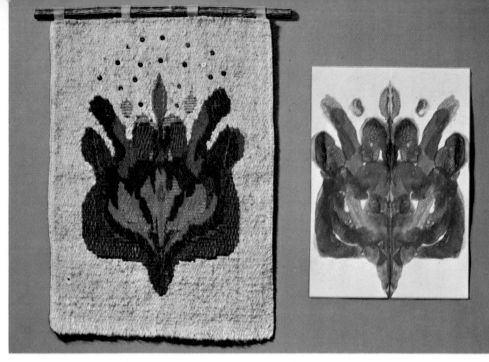

(Above) Decorative weave with sequins sewn on. The pattern has been obtained by means of squeezing a folded piece of paper on to which paint has been dabbed. (See also p. 79.) Designed and woven by Estine Östlund. (Below) The handbag on the left was woven according to a variation of the 'rose path' technique. (For instructions see p. 58.) The one on the right, woven in the Flemish way is based on a cutting exercise. (See p. 68.) The pattern for the purse is woven as above. (See also p. 79.)

The segments numbered 2 will be medium-dark in tone, but here the colour will be clearer and more distinct. The shaded segments are numbered 3. Each individual section can also be divided into two or three colours that are close together in hue and tone. It is advisable to divide the colours in the same way as in the illustration if you want to weave according to the Flemish technique from Skåne. The vertically striped sections correspond to 2 in tone, and the horizontally striped ones to 3.

If you want to weave with gradations between the different segments you must weave what are known as *hachures*. You can then achieve a very attractive effect by shading the background instead of dividing it into segments. (See the middle drawing.)

You can also draw veins on the leaves and weave with contrast colours. The leaves behind the top ones must be woven in a darker and bluer tone than the top ones. If you have drawn stems, they can be coloured light-brown or greenish-brown.

The third variation of the same pattern was done in an open-space weave with a semi-bleached linen warp, the weft yarn was semi-bleached tow yarn. Since it is meant to be used as a lampshade, the pattern will be seen with light behind it. In this case it is better to choose somewhat stronger colours for all three segments, as the white background and the luminosity of the lamp will automatically reduce the strength of the colours. The oranges were selected on the colour wheel: 1 is a reddish-yellow; 2 is a mid-colour in the orange quadrant; and 3 is more red than orange.

Pattern for a Flemish weave from Skåne.

Pattern for a tapestry weave from Skåne.

Pattern for the MMF technique.

77

(Left) A motif of fruit, woven by the MMF technique, makes an attractive window decoration. (Below right) The fruit motif woven by the technique of Flemish weaving from Skåne, with a background weave of diagonal joins. (Below left) Fruit motif woven with hachures and vertical pattern lines.

Rubbings

If you don't want to draw, you can make very satisfactory patterns by the technique known as *frottage*.

Collect some leaves or straws. Put them on to something hard and smooth, lay a thin piece of paper (such as flimsy typing paper) on top, and rub with a soft pencil or with a piece of lithographic chalk until the pattern has been transferred clearly on to the paper.

A pattern from the cross-section of a piece of wood was used for this frottage, *which was woven as a Finnish weave.*

Frottages *of various shapes of leaves.*

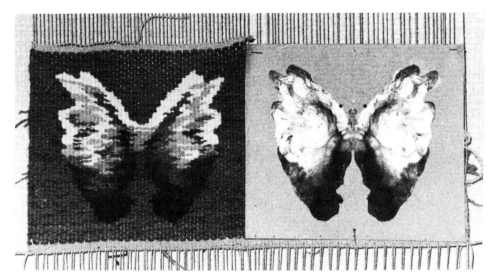

A butterfly pattern in black and white. The edges were not very clear and were cut off. Black, white, and grey are woven on a light-blue background. Designed and woven by Rut Holm.

Spontaneous patterns

You can create completely spontaneous patterns by dabbing paint on to a piece of paper, then folding it double and squeezing it. When you unfold the piece of paper you will find that you have a symmetrical design.

Variation: Dab some paint on to a piece of paper. Lay another sheet of paper on top and squeeze. Pull the top sheet off sideways, taking care not to lift it up.

Stylized pattern-making

Stylization involves simplification. You don't have to be good at sketching to make stylized patterns such as simplified flowers. Children automatically leave out any bit that isn't essential and draw the essential parts boldly and clearly. This is a particularly attractive way to create stylized patterns.

(Above left) Slightly stylized flowers in tapestry weave. Designed and woven by Rut Holm.

(Above right) The same flower stylized even further until it is suitable for the Finnish weaving technique. Designed and woven by Rut Holm.

(Below left) 'Bride's bread'. Woven on a loom. Designed and woven by Estine Östlund.

(Below right) You have to take extra care when colouring highly stylized shapes. Designed and woven by Elisabeth Hoppe.

Nature studies

You can use many different techniques to make nature studies, from a coarse rug weave to a clear transparent weave. These can be done in frames such as the 'Elisabeth' frame. You may even be able to invent your own techniques.

'Tree'. A bare tree on an island with pearls for fruit. Designed and woven by Rita Lundberg.

Techniques

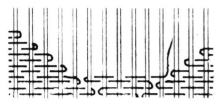

1. *Diagonal joining woven in sections.*

2. *Reversible röllakan.*

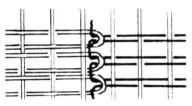

3. *One-sided röllakan.*

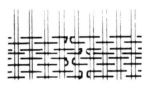

4. *Simple joining.*

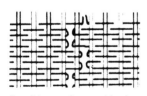

5. *'Norwegian teething'.*

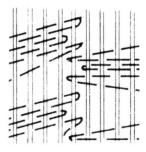

6. *Skåne teething.*

(Opposite) 'Lapp Witch'. Patterns derived from mythology and nature are combined in this hanging by Maija Kolsi-Mäkelä.

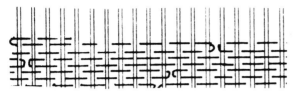

7. Hachures. *The colour 'streaks' are slotted into each other.*

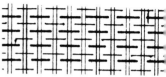

8. *Twist or double shuttle. Two colours are shot in alternatively and the stripes will run in the warp direction.*

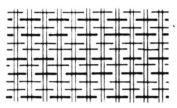

9. *Variation of twist.*

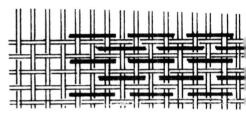

10. *'Russian' weave.*

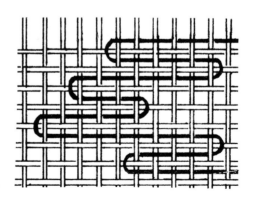

11. *The MMF technique, also known as the HV technique.*

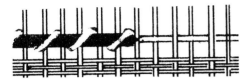

12. 'Nopp' weave. The pattern thread is weft-picked on to a stick to form loops.

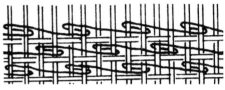

13. Snärj *weave.*

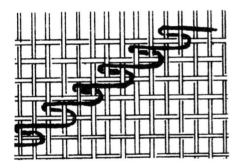

14. *Diagonal* Snärj *weave.*

15. Snärj *weave,* soumak *variation.*

Glossary of weaves

Crab weave
Picked extra weft-float pattern on a plain woven ground. Usually wool on linen warp. Based on irregular diagonal or diamond shaped units.

Double weave
The weaving of two cloths simultaneously one above the other and interlacing to form one cloth. The interlacing is often done in such a way that the design is the same on both sides but the colouring is reversed.

Finnish weave
A double weave with each cloth of a single different colour. A plain weave is used with sections being reversed to form the pattern.

Flemish weave
A tapestry technique derived from Flemish woollen tapestry on a linen warp. The weaver works at an upright loom with the reverse side of the work facing him.

MMF technique
Pattern made by putting in an extra weft thread for a short way between two ground weft threads and looping it back again freely at any point.

Röllakan weave
Tapestry weave with weft close beaten to cover warp.

Snärj technique
A form of tapestry weave in which the weft is looped round groups of warp threads at regular intervals; often not beaten down very closely in order to leave the looping visible.

List of suppliers

U.K. Suppliers

Looms

E. T. Bradley, 82 North Lane, East Preston, Sussex BN16 1HE.
Dryad Handicrafts, Northgate, Leicester.
Eliza Leadbeater, Granville House, 6 Granville Street, Winsford, Cheshire CW7 1DP.
Handweavers Studio & Gallery Ltd., 29 Haroldstone Road, London E17 7AN.

Swedish Looms

Bobby's Bookshop, 165 Linthorpe Road, Middlesbrough, Yorks.

Yarns

T. M. Hunter Ltd., Brora, Sutherland.
J. Hyslop Bathgate & Co., Victoria Works, Galashiels, TD1 1NY, Scotland.
Mersey Yarns, 2 Staplands Road, Liverpool L14 3LL.
Texere Yarns, 9 Peckover Street, Bradford 1.
Yarns, 21 Postland Street, Taunton TA1 1VY.
Handweavers Studio & Gallery Ltd., 29 Haroldstone Road, London E17 7AN.

U.S. Suppliers

Yarns and Looms

Fiber to Fabric, 317 Fourth Street, Kirkland, Washington 98033.
Lily Mills, Dpt. HWH, Shelby, North Carolina 28150.
Magnolia Weaving, 2635 29th West Seattle, Washington 98199.
Greentree Ranch Wools, 163 North Carter Lake Road, Loveland, Colorado 80537.
Nilus LeClerc, Inc., L'Islet, Quebec, Canada.
Robin and Russ, Handweavers, 533 North Adams Street, McMinneville, Oregon.
The Yarn Depot, Inc., 545 Sutter Street, San Francisco, California 94102.

Yarns

Contessa Yarns, Dept. HW, PO Box 37, Lebanon, Conn. 06349.

Looms

Schacht Spindle Company, 1708 Walnut Street, Boulder, Colorado.
Morgan Inkle Loom Factory, Railroad Engine House, Guilford, Connecticut 06437.

Index

Artist's frame 9

Chain stitch *9*, 25
coat fabric 43, 44, 58
colour 31—38
colour:
    circle 31, *32*
    combinations 33
    complementary 34
    foundation 31
    hue 32, 33
    interaction 34
    octants 32
    order of 31
    properties of 31
    rainbow 31
    rules of 38
    scale 33
    segments 32
    theories 31, 33
    transposition 37
    wheel *34*, 77
curtains 51, 57
curtains:
    linen 57

Design 26
design:
    colour in 30
    imagination in 30
double weave 46, 61—62
double weave:
    in a frame 66
    reversible 61
    reversible patterned 65
    variations in a frame 67
dress fabric 42

'Elisabeth' frame 9

Finishing processes 23
frames 8, *8*, *9*, 24, 25

Handbags *76*
hopsack weave 41

Lampshade *75*
leash sticks 15—16
leashing 16
light induction *34*
loom:
    collapsible *6*, 7
    small 7
    vertical tapestry 8, *9*

Moth-proofing 23
'monk's belt' 50
MMF technique 51

Nature studies 83, *84*

Panama cloth 41
pattern:
    cutting 28
    cutting exercise 72
    cutting out in black and white 68—71
    principles of 29
pattern ideas 68
pattern making 26—30
pattern variations 27
plaid 46
plaid:
    double-woven 47
poncho:
    double-woven 47, *53*

Reed settings 40
'rose path' theme 57, 59
rubbings 79, *80*

Scarf 44, 45
shawl 45, 46
shed:
    changing the 14, 15
skirt 43
skirt fabric 43, 44
spreading 13, 14
suit fabric 43—44, 58

Table mat 40
table runner 57
tapestry beater *25*

tapestry weave 8, 59
top-tying 21

Under-tying 21

Wall decoration *17*
wall-hanging 59, *75*
warp:
    basic 48, 49
    pulling on the 14
warping 11
warping:
    in the frame 24
    with four threads *12*
weave:
    setting up the 11
    double 46
weaving:
    in the bottom warp 63—64
    variations in techniques 39—67
weft-picked damask 60
window blinds 51
woollen weaves 42

Yarn calculation 10
yarn:
    standard numbers 10